THE INTEGRATED MAN

a map for modern manhood

First published in 2017 by Dane Tomas
Lennox Head NSW 2478

This book is a SpiritCast Network Book

National Library of Australia Cataloguing-in-Publication data:

Author:
Tomas, Dane
Title:
The Integrated Man
ISBN:
978-1975900250
ISBN-10:
1975900251
Subjects:
masculinity, self development, archetypes

Editor-in-chief: Cherise Lily Nana
Cover Design: Bliss Inventive

"Manliness consists not in bluff, bravado or loneliness. It consists in daring to do the right thing and facing consequences whether it is in matters social, political or other. It consists in deeds not words."

—Mahatma Gandhi

CONTENTS

Imagine you're a caterpillar. For your entire life you've been driven by the same basic drives: Eat, grow as big as possible and avoid predators. It's a simple existence. Climb up plant stems and seek out juicy green leaves. Eat them. Grow fat. Rinse and repeat.

Then one day a new impulse arises. New chemicals are secreted. The drive to build a cocoon takes over. You channel all of your resources into this activity, not knowing why but knowing that change is coming. Knowing that you cannot know the thing that comes next.

You also know that the old you has to die, before the new thing–the thing you cannot conceive or comprehend–can emerge.

And so you create a space in which you can conceal yourself from the world and completely disassemble everything you've ever been, in order for something new to emerge.

The process is painful. It is uncomfortable and uncertain, yet it has to take place if you are to become what you are destined to be.

If you're going to evolve, you must take a long, thorough look at yourself and let the obsolete parts fall away.

From the outside view, all is quiet.

Nothing is happening.

You are still, cocooned up inside a shelter of your own making.

Inside, however, you are dying.

The entity you thought you were: the simple, leaf munching, nutrient absorbing machine is no more.

Eventually, after the right period of time has passed you emerge...

You emerge as a completely new being and you take flight.

This is how successful initiation works.

WARNING:

This book has been written with the intention of delivering a powerful initiation.

If you choose to open yourself to the concepts inside, things will begin to change and there will be no going back.

INTRO: The Integrated Man

There's a war going on

Masculinity seems like a dirty word these days.

Switch on the TV and watch any sitcom or beer ad.

The men are depicted either as sexually incompetent, socially dysfunctional idiots OR as square-jawed killers with perfect abdominal muscles.

It seems like two options are presented:

Be a "hard man" who plays football, drinks beer, is somewhat sexist and loves cars OR be a "soft man" who is into art and feelings and who's been brainwashed by a feminist agenda.

The first lacks depth and sensitivity.

The second seems to feel the need to apologize just for having a penis.

The stereotypes might differ depending on where you've grown up and what circles you hang out in but... the message is similar.

Certain things are manly and certain things aren't.

At the same time, the society that birthed these rigid categories no longer exists.

During the '60s a revolution took place in the world's developed countries. Women broke out of the narrow roles that had confined them for hundreds of thousands of years and gradually expanded into territory that had been typically dominated by men.

This was a huge and necessary evolutionary step for humans as a species and it's my view that this dissolution of certain roles and categories has also plunged society into a certain level of confusion.

Ask any jaded old bloke with a couple of divorces under his belt: In the old days it was simple – men acted like this and women acted like that.

It was horribly constrictive but it provided a simple, clear social structure to navigate. (As long as you were heterosexual, able-bodied and satisfied with your station in life, obviously!)

So we could say that women claimed permission to access their masculine energy.

They began making money, assuming positions of leadership, and generally getting shit done.

From where I'm sitting, no corresponding revolution has yet happened for men – in fact, if anything, men are actively discouraged from being either too masculine (scary!) or too feminine (weak!).

What does that leave?

A generation of neutralized men!?

Fuck that!

In some of the social circles I hang out in, women do workshops about "how to connect with your inner goddess".

Meanwhile the work targeted toward men is attempting to tackle issues related depression and suicide.

So while the women were busily becoming CEOS and goddesses, what the fuck happened to us?

Well... we moved on from the old '50s stereotypical male who was tough, felt no emotion and brought home the bacon but... what else did we put in its place?

When I talk to men it seems we're not sure.

It seems that schools, the media, politically correct parents and many other influential forces want to reinforce this neutralized masculinity.

I don't believe it has to be this way. I've seen plenty of evidence that a man can cultivate all aspects of himself and be a complete and potent being – capable of a whole range of behaviour without having to in any way become "less of a man" to do it.

This book is about just that–how to become the most complete version of yourself.

And, if you're a woman reading this–I invite you to use this book to develop and integrate your own masculine side!

Welcome to The Integrated Man.

Lost at Sea

So how could it be that we have a couple of generations of men that have NO fucking clue how to actually BE men?

Then again, how could it be any other way?

We aren't shown.

There's no kind of pathway.

It's just expected that we know what to do.

And for the most part–we don't!

Many men have no fathers and the rest of us have fathers who also weren't shown how to be men. Young boys are largely raised by their mums, who cannot teach them what they need to know.

So we compete with other boys in the playground and we absorb tiny scraps of masculinity from comic book heroes and fictional characters in movies, but for the most part, this doesn't do the job.

I know, because I'm a man who's faced his own struggles and I speak with men regularly about these issues.

Not just a handful, I've spoken to and listened to HUNDREDS of men and what I hear is that many of us:

- have no direction. We don't know why we're here or have any sense of where we're going. This robs us of a huge amount of power and certainty about who we are.

- do not know how to relate to women because we are completely disconnected from our own feminine. This makes intimacy difficult and turns sex into a desperate quest for validation. Which in turn makes us terrible lovers!

- do not have an accurate picture of our strengths and weaknesses. This means we are completely unrealistic in what we think we can achieve in life, which leads to great disappointment. It also means we undervalue our natural talents and rarely achieve the success we could have.

- are terrified of our dark side. We fear our own aggression and killer instinct even though we (and the women in our lives) actually crave it. This leaves us feeling weak and leading boring, sanitized lives.

- cannot handle our emotions and feelings. My heart breaks when I think of the number of men who kill themselves each year just because they've never learned how to feel and process their emotions.

- can't just "get shit done". We struggle to engage our warrior energy, smash through obstacles and simply EXECUTE. This severely limits what we can achieve and experience in life.

- we don't accept (let alone love) ourselves for who we are. We're constantly striving to be someone else. This eats away at self-esteem and keeps us dissatisfied and disconnected.

None of these are necessary. It IS possible to reflect on what is and isn't working in our lives and change it. And that's what this book is for.

After twenty years of studying men and masculinity (starting with myself and eventually running programs and men's circles and speaking/listening to THOUSANDS of men), I've come to 2 conclusions:

1. Telling men what to do is useless.

2. Men will, however, use maps and we will solve problems for ourselves IF given the right tools.

So that's the approach I've taken with this book.

I'm not here to tell you that you SHOULD be "more" anything.

Not more masculine or more feminine.

Not more mental or more emotional or more physical or more spiritual.

Not more "alpha" or more "beta".

I'm just providing you with some pieces you can use however you see fit.

If you want:

- better connection with women and more sexual confidence
- more power and productivity
- more direction and purpose
- a deeper sense of love and acceptance and worthiness
- to embrace your dark side
- to be able to feel and express your feelings
- to understand your strength and weaknesses

then this book can help.

"You were born with balls for a reason..."

This comment struck me so much that I can still remember it now.

I was twenty-nine and had opted in for a free session with a relationship coach. This was the first thing she said to me.

I'd been single for about 5 years, and despite having an active sex life I found it impossible to stay in a relationship for more than a few weeks.

I also struggled to connect to the women I REALLY wanted to be with and at the time, I had no idea why.

Looking back on it, the issue was much more about PURPOSE; I hadn't yet committed to any kind of direction in life so why would I commit to a partner?

Attempting to solve my issues around sex, relationship, wealth and life purpose–and ultimately to have a healthy connection to my masculine and feminine sides– became a mission that would consume my life and take me on some seriously WEIRD adventures.

In 2013, I started dating Vanessa, an amazing woman who would influence my life in a big way over the next few years.

Roughly at the same time we met she started Dancing Eros–a project for women to explore their sexuality through dance and embodiment.

It was based around feminine archetypes and it was really fucking powerful.

I'd done some workshops working with masculine archetypes before but they'd mostly been about learning new ideas and ways of thinking.

Dancing Eros was something different. The archetypes Vanessa was working with were INITIATING her.

Each time she came into contact with one of them, she would change and grow– particularly in her relationship to herself as a woman.

It was amazing to witness and I decided I wanted the same thing for myself, except with the masculine equivalent.

Armed with a copy of *King, Warrior, Magician, Lover*, I started working through the masculine archetypes.

I'd set myself challenges that I thought would initiate me into the powers of each archetype.

What struck me was how powerful they were.

I dedicated a week to "being a king" which, to me at the time, was about wealth, integrity and organization.

A bunch of crazy shit happened.

All of a sudden people started hitting me up for money I owed them. Dramas between me and my family surfaced. It was quite unpleasant but I was smart enough to realize–oh these are all the things I have to handle if I want to be a king.

I went on to run the first Integrated Man Courses in 2014.

We took twelve men on an eight week journey through seven archetypes (the beast, the lover, the warrior, the king, the poet, the magician and the god). We also sat in a men's circle once a week and went through an emotional clearing process I'd created called The Spiral.

It was intense! Numerous men told me that in years of personal development they'd never experienced anything this powerful.

So I continued working with my own unique combination of archetypes for the next couple of years. When I decided to write this book, I knew I needed to go a little deeper if it was going to have any power.

So...

this is one of the craziest things I've ever done. As a guy who struggles to stick with a 21-day challenge (seven days is about good for me), if you told me I'd dedicate the best part of a year to journaling every day about these different energies, I would've told you you were mad–but I felt a real pull to do it.

Really this all began because it became obvious to me that I was skilled and talented in some areas and really limited in others.

I could sell thousands of dollars worth of workshops but I wasn't very physically strong.

I'd reach a point where I felt confident sexually but anything to do with romance or intimacy made me feel embarrassed.

I could discuss the mystical laws of the universe for hours but cooking 3 meals a day ad going to bed before 2 a.m. has eluded me my whole life.

Overall, I felt imbalanced. I'd done so much work to grow and evolve over the years and in general I liked myself and loved myself as a person (or so I thought), but it just seemed like the areas that were weak would forever prevent me from being the kind of man that I wanted to be.

A huge amount of this was in relationship to women. There were so many areas in which I felt "not good enough" and these would come up inside my relationship or when I was single and approaching women.

Many self-help and spiritual type books would say, "Just accept yourself," and, "You're perfect as you are," and I believe there's a place for this way of thinking but... it's not very masculine. The man in me wants to improve, to grow, to become more and to expand and I figured if I used this system of archetypes to look at myself holistically, at least I would grow in a balanced way.

So... I designed a rough journey.

I allocated roughly three weeks for each archetype and I committed to reading certain books, watching certain movies, setting up an altar dedicated to each archetype, committing to certain activities and journaling through all of it.

I created a seven-month archetype challenge for myself where I would do my best to live each month in the energy of each archetype:

The Beast – the physical body and connection to earth.
The Lover – charisma, sensuality, sexuality, feeling and flow.
The Warrior – focus, discipline and determination.

The King – integrity, wealth, organization and legacy.
The Poet – creativity, expression and leadership.
The Magician – mental intelligence, vision and transformation.
The God – transcendence, oneness and consciousness.

After the whole thing was done I added another archetype that had been there the whole time:

The Inner Child – innocence, vulnerability and self-nurturing.

So what the hell are archetypes anyway?

It's a word borrowed from Swiss psychologist, Carl Jung.

Jung was a genius, the father of Analytical Psychology and one of the first people to place any scientific importance on the inner world, dreams and the unconscious mind.

He used the word archetype to mean an "original type".

In other words, a primitive idea that we inherit from our earliest ancestors.

The idea is that the archetypes are already IN us.

We don't have to learn them–every child knows what "mother" and "father" means.

They are the original blueprints for femininity and masculinity.

In the 70s, the book *King, Warrior, Magician, Lover* came out. It explained 4 "masculine archetypes", which are the original energies I began working with years ago.

What struck me was how just talking about them and thinking about them allowed me to step into new parts of myself.

The book wasn't very practical. It didn't really tell you how to BECOME a king so I started making up experiments and initiations (more on initiation in a moment) that were designed to activate these energies inside me.

I found that simply placing a statue in my room on an altar would have a profound effect on my psyche. I'd be thinking about and feeling what that symbol meant to me all the time, even when I slept. I started watching movies that had the archetypes in them and noticing my responses to them. I started doing physical activities that put me into certain states of being, such as dancing, to get into my lover or lifting heavy weights to get me into my "beast" energy.

I also started journaling about them, and this may have been the most powerful thing.

What is an integrated man?

When I first put the program together I had to put a name on it so I could call people and sell it. Without even thinking about it I called it, "The Integrated Man".

The further we journeyed with this name the more it seemed perfect.

The word "integral" means that something is whole, complete and aligned across many levels. That's what I'd been aiming to grow into as a man.

I'd met so many men who were developed in one area but not in others.

The guys who were great with women were all broke.

The business dudes who made heaps of money were out of shape.

The guys who could hunt and track a deer and survive in the woods had no social skills, and the physically fit, alpha male dudes were completely out of touch with their emotions.

It seemed like there were lots of models of what masculinity could look like–but none of them seemed complete.

When I first started working with the different archetypes it became obvious to me that once you step into a certain character, it just takes you over. It really is like a kind of witchcraft.

Once you're under the influence of that particular character you start facing your fears and learning new things FAST.

I got the crazy idea that if I did enough work with these energies I could develop really quickly, even in areas where I'd been hopeless for most of my life.

It was exciting, like that scene in The Matrix where Neo says, "I know Kung Fu." It was as if the archetype was a new software that could be downloaded into my system.

I should be clear with this; the goal isn't to become perfect.

I'm definitely not any kind of superman – I'm just a regular dude. Bu what I have seen in several years of stepping in and out of these different characters is that I'm becoming more well-rounded and more able to experience all kinds of things that used to be WAY outside my comfort zone.

IF YOU'RE STILL WITH ME... then you've probably realized that we're undertaking a journey together and there's no turning back now!

If we're going to do this, to start stepping into new parts of ourselves and taking on new practices in order to develop into better men, there are a few ideas I'd like to share with you that can really help.

The thing with this work is, it can bring up your stuff. We've lived our life up to this point by forming certain habits and, as freeing as it can be to step out of those habits, it can also be very difficult. After all, the way we've done things up until now has kept us safe right?

In the next section: Maps & Tools, I'm going to break down some of the ideas and concepts that have helped me navigate some of the crazy experiences that I've stumbled into in pursuit of this goal of become a more "integrated man".

How to best use this book

This book has been written not just to be read but to be ABSORBED. I've done my best to take the initiations and transformations I've gone through and distill them into a magic potion that you can drink and receive the benefits of.

Some sections contain stories or metaphors, these have been carefully chosen to talk to your unconscious mind. If you open yourself now to receive them then you may start to notice various things happening in your life. You might have dreams. You might notice new opportunities standing out to you. You might even feel the urge to make up or create new habits or rituals or routines, or do some things completely out of the ordinary.

If you surrender to these urges then you will find yourself stepping into a whole new world.

If you want to receive more active transformation from this book, after reading the short stories just pause for a few moments, feel the new information sinking in and trust that you cannot UNLEARN this stuff.

Our whole society is built on myths and legends. Stories are the software on which our brain runs. If you open yourself to receive these more deeply you will begin to reorganize the parts of you that need healing and upgrading.

Other sections of the book will contain checklists or short quizzes.

Each checklist is an opportunity to do a quick but deep self-assessment.

It may be worth sitting with and feeling into the questions before answering them.

Or you might like to journal a whole page on each question and see what comes out.

THE ONLINE COURSE:

This book has been designed so that you can use it by itself OR you can use it in conjunction with the online version of The Integrated Man archetype challenge.

I've built this challenge based around the format I use but packaged into an eight-week course.

This will give you step-by-step instructions on how to initiate yourself into whichever energies you choose so that you can become a stronger, more expressive, more confident and whole version of yourself.

You'll be guided each week and will share your experiences with other men in a private group. We'll look shortly at the massive impact being part of a community of other men has on us.

If you want to participate in the online course (it's only $47 AUD) click the link here and go to www.theintegratedman.com

MAPS & TOOLS

I've met enough really kick-ass twenty-somethings and enough completely lost fifty-year-old boy-men to realize that manhood ISN'T something that just automatically happens with age.

We can blame all kinds of causes for this, ranging from the industrial revolution creating a world where boys no longer work alongside their father like they did in the old days, to radical feminism, which demonizes masculinity and "the patriarchy" as evil.

Whether these things are genuinely to blame for men's current predicament or not doesn't matter. What I'm interested in doing is offering men maps and tools to navigate the path ahead and tackle the obstacles that we'll face as we move forward.

If we want to develop ourselves consciously there are 5 main things we need to be able to do:

1. Decide where it is we actually want to get to

Who do you want to be? What skills and qualities do you want to possess? What results would you like in your life? So few people ask themselves these questions and so few people end up living the sort of life that is genuinely fulfilling and meaningful.

In the "Lifestyle Design" section at the end of this chapter I'll teach you a basic system for mapping out how you want your life to be and then show you how to use the archetypes to help you develop the new qualities and skills you'll need to get there.

2. Look at your current situation honestly

This may be the hardest and most confrontational step. The checklists in this book are designed to help in this area. Really, though, it's just about getting honest. What areas of your life are you not happy with? What issues have you not addressed? This is different from beating yourself up. It's done with an attitude of knowing, "If I can name it, I can change it."

3. Diagnose

This is where the archetypes can be very useful. If we start stepping into "Warrior" type experiences and we don't have a lot of determination, discipline, focus or mental toughness, we're going to come face-to-face with this very quickly, usually in the form of uncomfortable feelings and a desire to run away!

4. We need to be able to find teachers or tools or experiences to initiate us

This is a skill in itself and it's my intention that this book can give you some leads (at least by linking you to other books and organizations), as well as teach you a new language and set you up with things to google (e.g. "What is a lingham massage?")

5. We need to be able to integrate our learnings into our bodies and into our lives

Going on retreats, doing workshops and making up crazy challenges can be fun and rewarding but the real magic is in bringing these new skills into our daily lives. This is my favorite part. The first time I deadlifted my own body weight happened during the beast archetype challenge. That's a permanent physical and real change. That goal might mean very little to someone who's been physically strong and athletic their whole life, but for me, a guy who's largely avoided exercise and sport–hitting this benchmark signified a HUGE landmark. It meant that I became more grounded, solid and strong and the impacts of that in other areas–such as my sex life, my business and my day-to-day confidence–were profound.

Likewise, if you used to freeze inside when you approached a woman–the day you realize you are calm, cool and collected in a situation that used to terrify you is an amazing one. Get clear on what you want to create in your normal, everyday life and use these outcomes as benchmarks.

I think of the work that has to be done as falling into two categories:

1. Facing dragons
2. Developing skills

FACING DRAGONS

This really means looking at parts of ourselves that we don't want to look at and dealing with the difficult, unresolved parts of our life. This often involves revisiting past injuries and events, and then resolving and integrating them.

A large part of my work (outside of the Integrated Man project) has been in creating and teaching tools to help people process emotional baggage and clear their blocks.

One of these is what I just call, "Clearing your shit." I packaged up a particular way of doing this that you can learn from my book *Clear Your Shit* and there are training videos for free online at:

www.clearyourshit.com

When it comes to facing dragons, the more we do it the easier it gets. Clearing helps because we're all loaded up with what I call "conditioning"– that is, beliefs and emotional patterns that are handed down from one generation to the next. Many of us have behaviors and habits that we did not choose–things that we do unconsciously and we don't even know why!

This drove me nuts for years.

In my early twenties I learned kinesiology and found it to be a useful (but complicated) process for releasing emotional blocks from the body. Eventually I repackaged this tool into a new modality that you can learn quickly and for free.

In addition to the basic clearing tools I also created a process called The Spiral. This is like the granddaddy of all transformation journeys–the original Integrated Man program combined The Spiral with the masculine archetypes you're going to learn about shortly.

The beauty of learning clearing and going through The Spiral is that, once all that crap is out of the way, you won't get so stuck in negative feelings anymore. You'll still feel them but you'll be able to REALLY feel them, get the lesson and then let them go.

The other process that helps me with Facing Dragons is journaling:

The more successful people I get to work with, the more I realize how many of them journal daily. For me, masculinity, archetype work and journaling go hand-in-hand. Mainly because it's an awesome way to get in touch with what's beneath the surface.

For many men, we've been trained NOT to feel our emotions and this single thing is one of the areas that keeps us numb, clueless and disempowered. Simply journaling each day begins to build a bridge between who we are on the conscious level and who we are deep down. Even journaling each day for a week can heal old wounds and open up entire new dimensions to who we are.

Used in conjunction with archetypes, journaling is even more powerful. Say you decide to work on your "lover" energy for a month. The first thing I would suggest is write down all your intentions of who you want to become, what you want to explore and what results you'd like. From there, keeping a daily "lover" journal will bring your focus deeply onto the areas of your life affected by The Lover. Emotions will arise, you'll start to see patterns of behavior that affect your love life and within a few days you'll be more in touch with The Lover than you ever have in your life.

Journaling is such a powerful way to organize our thoughts, unpack our deep feelings and get to know ourselves and I recommend it as a way to work through this book.

SKILL DEVELOPMENT:

Evolving as men isn't ALL about facing our shit. The other part of the equation is getting good at stuff! Most of us are born with certain talents and we develop our skill-sets as we get older. What I didn't realize until much later on in life is that ALMOST EVERYTHING IS A SKILL.

Typically, men learn sports or play guitar and pick up some skills that go hand in hand with our personalities and that we're naturally good at. This is usually done without any kind of overall plan and by the time a man is forty years old, he may realize he's good at some stuff and not so good elsewhere.

This is fine, I suppose. I wanted something more than that though. There were so many areas that I assumed were fixed. For years I was awkward and shy around women. ESPECIALLY around women I found very attractive. As I became more successful as a rapper in my twenties I began to realize that women were approaching me more and more often and that was fun, but I also knew I'd never really addressed my underlying problem–I didn't know what to do or how to act when I wanted to connect with a woman I was attracted to.

Eventually I realized meeting women was a learnable skill. I spent time with men who were successful in this area of their lives and took notice of the ways in which they behaved that were different to me. I started going to places where no one knew me and approaching beautiful women. I read books on the subject. Gradually I immersed myself in this pursuit. Slowly and surely I got better at it, I got confident and I started to be able to meet women that I was attracted to and connect with them easily and effortlessly.

This was mind-blowing to me. I'd always believed that some guys were good in that area and some guys weren't. Once that was proved untrue I started asking:

"What others things are learnable skills?"

I realized I'd been terrible with money my whole life. I suppose I'd believed that some people are rich and some people aren't and that's just how it is. I decided to challenge this belief too. I started going to courses, reading books and hanging out in environments where wealthier people spent time. Gradually it started changing my attitude about a whole range of subjects. I started learning about sales, marketing, money, business, investing and so on.

Eventually my results started to change. In 2012 I quit my telemarketing job and started my first real business. Within a year I was making my old yearly wage EVERY SINGLE MONTH.

One by one, I've been able to turn areas of weakness into strengths.

The fastest way I know of doing this is by:

STEPPING INTO THE CHARACTER OF SOMEONE WHO ALREADY HAS THE SKILLS THAT I WANT.

This is where the archetypes come in. Really, each archetype is a sort of character or a role that we can step into, rather than just PRETENDING however, there is something about archetypes that will take over if you let them.

When you step into your WARRIOR you're not just "pretending" to be a warrior. You're actually activating a deep part of yourself that was always there.

That's the magic here–this idea that we can tap into a primal force that's bigger than us that already knows everything we want to know.

Many men share this experience of becoming fathers. They don't know what it is they're supposed to do exactly but something about stepping into the ROLE of the father makes them become one.

So, we can use this knowledge as a way to rapidly speed up our development as men.

More on this in the next chapter. First there are a few more ideas I'd like to share with you that will drastically change how you view the world.

INITIATION

Initiation means to begin. More specifically, when used in a tribal or ceremonial context it's the intentional act of transitioning a person from one stage of their life to another.

It can also have the connotation of calling down a new power or giving someone access to secret knowledge.

Since the dawn of time women have been initiated by their bodies. The stages maiden, mother and crone are clearly marked by the biological transformations that take place at the onset of menstruation, by childbirth and at menopause.

So even though it's true that women have also lost their way a little in this world of changing roles and meanings, on some level women are still initiated into wisdom by their bodies.

Men, on the other hand, don't go through the same level of physical transformation and in various indigenous cultures different masculine initiations were developed–most notably to mark the transition from boy to man.

Initiation typically goes through several basic stages:

1. Separation

In the classic tribal boyhood initiation this usually means separation from the village and the family and–most significantly–separation from the mother. Up until this point the boy has been under the mother's protection and nurturance. He has not yet had to face the realities of the world.

2. Enter the underworld

Then, one night, the elders arrive at the door and take the boy away from his mother on a journey into something completely unknown. He doesn't know the full extent of what's coming. On the walk into the forest or to the sacred spot his fears will arise and he will have to face them.

3. Face pain/hardship/ego death

Depending on the tradition the boy may have to hunt and kill a wild animal, suffer some pain inflicted on him by an elder, face isolation in the wilderness, consume a psychedelic plant medicine or in some other way be initiated by a force greater than himself.

The general theme is that something sufficiently strong enough to destroy the boy's identity will occur. The fear or the pain or the potency of the experience will take over and the boy will have to surrender to it. In a sense, he will die. The person who left to go on the adventure is not the one who returns home. He BECOMES someone else.

4. Return home with new power

After the experience is complete the boy will return home and he will be recognized as a man. He will adopt a new role in the social structure of the community. He will be tasked with new responsibilities such as protection of the village, hunting food etc. His mother will no longer relate to him as her little boy. He will internally and externally be recognized as a man.

This marking of the transition from boy to man creates an orderly structure to give the individual an extremely clear context for understanding his place in society.

It's commonly suggested by behavioral psychologists and beardy men's work dudes alike that the lack of initiation in our society is a significant part of why modern day men don't know what the fuck's going on.

Feminist theory, on the other hand, suggests that "toxic masculinity" is to blame for men's problems–in other words, that the rigid roles enforced on men are responsible for much of the dysfunction we're now facing.

Personally I think there's a little bit of truth in both of these ideas.

Either way you look at it–the problem is identity.

We have no idea WHO we're supposed to be and what roles we're supposed to play in the society we live in.

I've sat in hundreds of men's circles, sessions with men and group settings where men share their wins, challenges, learnings and innermost feelings.

One of the most common things that comes up is this sense of there being no official marker for the day we become men.

Is it when we first have sex? When we get our first job? When we have our first fight? When we become fathers? When our bodies grow hair?

Many men have a lack of clarity about WHEN they became men or IF they ever did.

This was not so in older societies.

This doesn't mean that the old style of initiation will solve all of our problems.

Being lead into the forest and having his grandfather cut a piece of his cock off isn't going to help the average inner city youth make sense of his life.

What seems clear to me is that we need to find ways of INITIATING OURSELVES that are appropriate to the world we live in and that help us become the kind of men WE want to become.

So whether you're a young man wanting to make sense of it all or you're sixty-five years old and you're wanting to heal some boyhood pieces that are STILL floating around, I believe this knowledge can be helpful, especially if we combine it with the archetypes.

One last thing about initiation…

I've noticed that the events of our life initiate us in the ways that we need. We experience opportunities for initiation all the time. Things happen that mark the stages between one stage and another but… many of those events don't cleanly make sense in our lives.

I was involved in a violent incident when I was sixteen.

I was bullied and stabbed another boy with a knife.

It was serious and turned my (and I assume his) world upside down.

It was an initiation of sorts, but a very negatively charged, unconscious one that would take me years to process and unpack.

Michael Brown, author of *Alchemy of the Heart*, describes initiation like this:

Conscious initiation brings greater integration.

Unconscious initiation brings more disintegration.

Much of my work as a coach and facilitator using various emotional healing tools has been to help people revisit traumatic events and release the emotional charge or negative meanings associated to the event.

For example, my experience of the stabbing taught me some positives:

That if I stand up for myself I get respected.

That I am powerful.

It also taught me that asserting my boundaries was extremely dangerous and could cause harm and threaten my freedom. Until I was able to let go of the trauma and unconscious beliefs created by this experience, it was very hard for me to fully channel my WARRIOR energy in a safe way!

In the archetype section (it's coming soon I promise!) you're going to learn how to bring certain character types into your life that will provide you with some of the initiations you never received.

This is a really powerful way to unlock aspects of yourself that may never be developed unless you seek out the right sorts of experiences to awaken them.

I also highly recommend signing up for the online version of The Integrated Man Archetype Challenge here: www.theintegratedman.com

STAGES OF MASCULINE DEVELOPMENT

Many men live their life not knowing where they are going or where they have come from.

They lack a big picture overview that could help them understand who they are, what areas they are talented in and where they might need further development. Because of this, they tend to "stay in their lane", deriving satisfaction and meaning from only one or two areas in life (e.g. work or sports or their ability to pick up women) and as a result, life gradually becomes more meaningless over time.

I remember the first moment I began to understand that there were maps of human growth and evolution; visual representations of the different stages we go through in any journey.

This completely blew my mind. For the first time I had a location in my psyche. I could SEE where I'd come from, where I was now and where I was going. Even if the map was just an interpretation (which is all a map can ever be), I knew I had a sense of direction and a reference point to start from.

That can make all the difference between helplessness and confidence.

So if initiation is a TOOL that we can use to help us transition from one stage of life to another, it could be helpful to have some idea of what those stages might be!

I found the following map beneficial because it helped me realize that no matter how hard I work, or how smart I think I am, there's another type of development that DOES come with age.

Often as we are growing up as men we can be hard on ourselves, for example being a teenager and feeling depressed that we don't know what the purpose of our life is, or being in our thirties and worrying that we're not having enough fun and adventure.

The truth is, that as well as taking an active hand in our own development (which is what this book is about), it's also really helpful to know that men move through certain stages at certain ages.

This particular sequence comes from the book *Keys to the Kingdom* by Alison Armstrong.

Alison's books are written to help women understand men but I found that reading them as a man also gave me a lot of insight into how we think and act, and helped me be more accepting of myself.

She uses a medieval knight metaphor and calls the different stages:

The Page (age 0 to about thirteen)
The Knight (age thirteen to late twenties)
The Prince (early thirties to early forties)
The King (early forties to old age)

THE PAGE

The first stage a man goes through (as a boy) is a page. This stage lasts from birth to about thirteen years of age. During this stage boys dream of adventure and want to be good at things.

They gets frustrated when they can't master certain skills and constantly wants to take risks and test themselves. The primary mistake parents and teachers make with boys of this age is to try to get them to behave like girls (who are much easier to manage). This process of risk-taking and pushing boundaries is eventually what leads the page to become a knight.

THE KNIGHT

This stage lasts roughly from puberty to the late twenties. During this stage a man is driven by an intense need for adventure, challenge, conquest and fun. Knights are not usually preparing for the future and may not want to "commit". They may not be particularly inspired by "doing the right thing" or 'living their purpose." This is natural and healthy.

It can be helpful for women to understand that a man in this stage may not be ready for a serious relationship. Experiencing the Knight stage thoroughly will give a man the experiences he needs to know what he wants to do with his life. Missing out on this stage can lead to immaturity later on, and an older man may find himself needing to "go back" and have some of the adventures that he missed out on in his youth in order to properly mature.

THE PRINCE

This stage is all about building, creating and making a mark in the world. It runs from the late twenties all the way up to the early forties and is divided into three sub-stages.

EARLY PRINCE: This stage is all about deciding WHAT he will do. The man will try different things until he finds what fits and then he will make a decision.

MIDDLE PRINCE: Once decided, the man moves into middle prince. This stage can be all-consuming. Many women struggle with men in this stage because their focus will be more on life purpose and empire-building than on relationship and nurturing a family.

LATE PRINCE: This is described as a period of confidence and grace where the man can enjoy what he's accomplished and also experience other areas.

THE TUNNEL: Late prince doesn't last long and gives way to a painful transitional stage called "the tunnel".

At this point the prince will question his purpose, his identity and values. What he's been investing all his energy into may seem meaningless. This stage is often written off as a "mid-life crisis" but actually it's another initiation of sorts. The man will question who he is and what he stands for. When he comes out the other end he will emerge with a sense of, "This is who I am."

THE KING:

The king brings with him a new energy of masculine maturity and certainty of who he is. He will be far less changeable than the previous stages; by this point a man knows who he is and what he will and won't stand for. In this stage the man has far more resources to offer as a provider and nurturer and a much lower tolerance for bullshit. A man who has come solidly into his king energy will not be with a partner who doesn't admire and support him.

MY JOURNEY AND HOW THE ARCHETYPES HELP

Personally this framework helped me realize that I was not going insane as I transitioned from middle prince, to late prince and went through the tunnel. I wish I'd known about this in my twenties so I could have cut myself some slack and realized that I was "gathering information" about the world!

When I was in middle prince stage it was an intense, almost biological drive. I wanted to take over the world. When I went into the tunnel I questioned everything, I felt like everything I'd believed strongly was complete bullshit; my values turned on their head and I felt completely lost and purposeless.

It was at this point that I constructed the seven month version of the Integrated Man Archetype Challenge. I decided that if this stage of life was going to force me inwards to look at myself, I might as well go along with it and get as much value and growth from it as possible.

So I mapped out the different areas of my life and took a long, hard look at which areas I was doing really well (e.g. business, spirituality) and where I was struggling (intimate relationship, physical health, social life, creativity) and began setting challenges using the archetypes to initiate myself into the areas that didn't seem to have developed.

Thankfully, because of Alison Armstrong's stages of masculine development I had a sense that I was "in the tunnel" and that it wasn't permanent. Eventually I was going to come out of the other side! It wasn't a "midlife crisis" and I wasn't "going mad" (although I did feel like it a few times).

One of the differences between men and women is the fact that men go through this very linear series of developmental stages.

Despite the fact that the stages play out in order, I don't personally believe this ripening into KING energy is completely inevitable. I could sense in my mid-thirties that I didn't really have all of the right pieces in order to become the kind of man I wanted to be in my forties.

I was skinny and weak, I was disorganized in so many different ways and I'd been doing so many things to impress other people rather than to fulfill my own values.

As I went through the challenge, one by one I got to see the truth (faced my dragons) and develop new ways of doing things that set me up to be a more mature, more stable and powerful individual.

I realized this work could make up for some of the things I never learned when I was growing up and help me become the kind of man that I'd be proud to be!

THE MATURE MASCULINE MINDSET

If we're really going to step onto this challenging path of self-initiation, there are certain ways of looking at the world that can really impact whether or not we can handle what lies ahead.

Many people want to do great things and set out to challenge themselves but– without the right mindset–they are doomed to fail before they even start.

The following are some ideas that I've learned from twenty years of personal development that make it much easier to handle change and take control of our lives.

Some of them may at first seem unreasonable, ridiculous or unfair, but if you can try on some of these ideas (even just temporarily), you may find that you dramatically expand what you're capable of achieving in life.

BEGIN WITH THE END IN MIND.

This is the single most useful thing I can offer you when it comes to designing your life or approaching any kind of project.

It's the heart of all masculine strategy and problem-solving.

We start by asking, "What outcome do I want from this?" and then by clarifying what that looks like.

"I wanna feel confident," is not as useful as, "I want to be able to speak in front of large groups" or, "I want to be able to talk to attractive women" when it comes to designing a course of action.

Get the picture clear of what your outcomes are and all areas of your life will begin to improve. Who do you want to BE, what do you want to DO and what results do you want to HAVE.

When you have this part sorted, knowing what to do next is very easy. This is the central idea underneath the "life design" section at the end of the book, which is going to show you how to design exactly what you want.

ACT AS IF YOU ARE COMPLETELY RESPONSIBLE FOR EVERYTHING THAT HAPPENS.

People hate this one but I'm serious. I don't mean you personally are to blame for global warming–I mean that the circumstances of your life come down to you.

Drop the concept of blame completely. Whatever has happened, has happened. It's not your fault but.. it IS your responsibility. What does that mean? It means you're the one who gets to choose how you RESPOND to any event or circumstance.

It means you have to drop the luxury of blaming others. It's not your parents. It's not the government. It's not the girl who dumped you or that kid who bullied you. Those things still happened, obviously. I'm not talking about sticking your head in the sand, simply adopting the belief that YOU are the one who's responsible for what happens next.

From here on in YOU are responsible for the life you create, for the decisions you make and the results that come from them. No one else can create your life, only you.

EVERYTHING YOU EXPERIENCE IS IN SOME WAY A REFLECTION OF YOU.

Once again, there's no blame. When we start stepping into new roles, setting intentions and deciding we want to evolve–a lot of strange things start to happen. It helps if we can be curious and pay attention. Maybe we can ask the questions: "Why do things like that keep showing up?" and "What does it mean in my life?"

Once the archetype challenge is underway, each "flavor" seems to invite new events into our life. We commit to being a warrior and all of a sudden we have to confront the things we've been avoiding. We step into The Lover and our partner tells us she's sexually unsatisfied and we have to deal with our insecurities, OR we talk about being a King and suddenly all of our family challenges from childhood show up.

What I usually ask is: What does this reflect to me? Where's the mirror here? What's the common theme?

THERE IS NO FAILURE. ONLY FEEDBACK.

This one has stopped me from giving up thousands of times. So many times people step into something new and give up when it gets hard. I'm sorry to point it out but if you start doing this work LOTS of the things you step into will be things you SUCK at completely. That's where the growth is. Once we realize that every error, every awkward feeling, every criticism and every discomfort we face is a piece of useful information, everything gets a little easier.

If you are really underdeveloped in the area of your Lover then going on dates or learning massage or salsa dancing is probably going to be scary or uncomfortable at first. That's OK. The idea is to go, have experiences and then integrate the information. My favorite way is to journal, "What did I learn?" each time I have a new experience.

YOU ARE NOT BROKEN.

Can you hold the understanding that you are "fine as you are", while also working to learn about yourself and grow?

It seems like a paradox but I've found it to be the most functional way to move forward.

On one level, you are full of shit, have all kinds of weaknesses and things to "fix".

If we get a little deeper though, if we feel into our hearts and our bodies and get present in the moment, we realize that we are already complete.

There are wounds, there are conditioned patterns of behavior and there are skills we haven't developed yet. Beyond that, our "essence" is perfect right now. Learning to live in this paradox is part of being an integrated man.

If you need help to process unresolved emotions, trauma or blocks please go to www.clearyourshit.com and work through my free clearing program. It will help.

HOW YOU DO ANYTHING IS HOW YOU DO EVERYTHING.

Our minor habits tell the story of our life. Whether you dive into an activity that makes you uncomfortable or not. Whether you hold a woman's eye contact when you speak to her. Whether you slack off when you're 80% of the way through the task.

The micro holds the keys to the macro! With this we can observe ourselves when we undertake challenges.

What are the things that come up? Does this come up in other areas of life? Why did it happen? This ability to observe ourselves is the key to growth and transformation that actually takes us to where we want to go.

RESISTANCE IS A TEACHER

One of the biggest indicators that something is going to be a huge area of growth for me is... when it comes to the crunch, I really don't want to do it!

Resistance shows up in the form of making excuses, dropping off partway through a commitment, emotions of frustration and anger coming up or sometimes in the form of finding a new shiny thing to distract us from what we committed to.

Pay attention to it. Ask questions such as, "Could this be a sabotage pattern? What am I afraid will happen if I do this?"

Often we are more afraid of things that will change us than things that will keep us the same. I never had strong resistance to watching Netflix for hours.

I have had resistance to taking the steps that I KNOW will completely upgrade my whole life. See if you can pay attention to the feeling and DO THE THING ANYWAY.

THE MIND-BODY CONNECTION

So now we know how to initiate ourselves, what stages men go through, and how to think about life in a way that empowers us to keep moving forward.

The next question is, "How 'in your body' are you?"

Currently the biggest issues that face men are depression, anxiety and suicide. Most of us have been trained from childhood that "boys don't cry" and to "harden up".

The end result of this is generations of men who don't actually know what they feel.

This doesn't just make men numb. It stops us from being able to solve our problems. It disconnects us from our sexuality (because for most people being sexual brings up all kind of emotional vulnerability), and all of that unprocessed emotion restricts our ability to communicate.

I spent the first twenty years of my life trying to harden up and become as tough as I possibly could. Ironically, when I got really interested in sexuality and wanting to become a more skilled lover, I realized:

"My ability to feel, process and express my emotions is the key to mastery."

In the section entitled FACING DRAGONS I talked about using Clearing and Journaling to help resolve difficult feelings and emotions.

In addition to both of those tools, getting good at just FEELING what is going on inside ourselves is one of the keys to unlocking our power.

Knowing what's going on beneath the surface is a fine art, and one that can take a while to master.

Here are some of the practices (in addition to those I've already mentioned) that can help further develop the mind-body connection.

BODYWORK

One of the most powerful ways to get out of the head and into the body is by receiving bodywork such as massage, chiropractic and osteopathy. In addition to this, regular saunas and baths can help to soften the body and release the rigid patterns that we hold that prevent us from feeling.

For a more accelerated way to break through blocks around emotion and sex, you can seek out erotic massage or tantric lingham (cock) massage. This may take a little work (google "tantric massage") but when held by a skilled practitioner (rather than by a lover), this work can heal abuse trauma, re-pattern defense mechanisms and release emotional armor from the body.

All of the above can lead to increased self-connection, deeper self-love and permanent upgrades in knowing ourselves and our bodies.

MEDITATION

All styles of meditation can be beneficial. One of the most widely spread is Vipassana (literally meaning, "insight") meditation. This style of Buddhist meditation has been a very popular pathway for many men I know to become more conscious and aware individuals.

The Vipassana centers are established all over the world and run ten-day silent meditation retreats by donation. This practice is an excellent foundation for learning to "watch the mind" and become acquainted with our mental and emotional content.

CONSCIOUS DANCE

This one was initially one of the scarier ones for me as the prejudices I grew up with told me it "wasn't masculine" to dance. 5 RHYTHMS is a guided practice that takes place all over the world that uses freeform dance (meaning there are no "moves") as a way to connect you to your body and self-expression. Although dance can be seen as a "feminine" form of practice, I believe it's an invaluable way of unlocking our flow, creativity and freeing up the body to move more easily.

PSYCHEDELICS & PLANT MEDICINES

Although controversial because of their varying legal status in different countries, the use of psychedelics such as LSD, psilocybin mushrooms, Ayahuasca and DMT is increasing in popularity as a way to expand consciousness, resolve unconscious emotional issues and awaken deeper sensitivity and connection to planet earth.

MARTIAL ARTS

In general martial arts have been an amazing pathway for men to cultivate more presence, embodiment, awareness and confidence for millennia. Whether we're talking traditional marital arts like kung fu, karate, aikido or boxing, or more modern and popular martial arts like Brazilian Jiu Jitsu and MMA, there are huge benefits from engaging in live sparring and learning to fight as well as the increased body awareness and discipline that comes from learning new movement patterns.

COMMUNITY & CONNECTION

It's often said that masculinity isn't learned–it's transmitted.

So much of what we are trained to value as men are ruggedly individualistic values gained by solitary "us against the world" type struggles. Indeed, the masculine form of initiation typically takes place alone or is transmitted to us by one other person. However, outside of this, the best way to develop as men is to surround ourselves with other men that possess good qualities and that model healthy male behavior.

Again, one of the primary issues that face men is isolation. I believe this is because seeking help, being vulnerable or being intimate with others is culturally considered to be "unmasculine". Either we have to expand our definition of what masculinity is OR we can expand to understand that our feminine side is an equally important part of what it takes to be man.

Most men don't have access to a variety of healthy role models. Nor do we have access to brotherhood of a form that is non-judgmental and that gives permission to talk about ALL subjects and share our challenges.

Many of the men I've spoken to and worked with share the experience of having close connection with other men, usually though work or sports but have a limit to what they would feel comfortable sharing with those men. If they were to talk about specific subjects, such as sex (beyond the realm of boasting) or emotions or intimacy, the general consensus is that it would become awkward or not be accepted.

So most men either follow the example of the other members of their peer group and don't think about or talk about these issues OR they retreat and isolate themselves from the group in general.

Some of the biggest integrations and healings for me started when I began attending men's circles. I'd grown up in strong competition with other men, and the story that "I was different" had been deeply engrained into my psyche since early high school.

What blew me away was how many men shared their version of the same experience in the circles. Is it possible that all those boys I grew up disliking, afraid of and in competition with, were feeling many of the same things?

I thought it was just me. I realize now that many man feel like outsiders. That really shocked me.

Another side effect of the lack of brotherhood is that men rely heavily on women for connection (and connection in most cases means sex). Therefore having sex with women becomes this NEED rather than something beautiful, pleasurable and valuable to give as well as receive; it becomes almost like a lifeline.

This makes many men desperate, needy and even resentful of women. It also means we objectify them (and ourselves) because the whole interaction becomes about the goal of getting laid or getting a top up of feminine energy, rather than of sharing and expanding together.

So, in order to overcome this, in addition to solitary self-initiations and working away on our own, it's important to find ways to connect with other men who are open to sharing this journey of masculine awakening and growth.

MEN'S CIRCLES

The men's circle is a time-honored process that allows men to share a space where they can listen to one another and be heard in a non-judgmental, authentic and vulnerable space. I started attending these a few years ago and soon enough began running my own. They completely changed my relationship to other men. I realized that many of the fears and vulnerabilities I thought were unique to me were very similar to what other men were dealing with. I also began to feel safe and trusting around other men–something I never really experienced growing up. I realized that I'd been competing with every other man on the planet and that was exhausting. Depending on where you live there may be existing men's circles near you. If you can't find one please check out this resource on how to run a men's circle.

MEN'S GATHERINGS

A few years ago I was invited to run a workshop at an Australian men's gathering called Menergy. At that time I didn't really understand why I would want to go to a gathering solely for men. Eventually I went and it was absolutely transformational, to the point that I committed to go every year and encouraged other men to attend. There will be men's gatherings in your general area. Google "men's gatherings" and see what you can find!

ONLINE COMMUNITY

The integrated men's circle online can be found here:

https://www.facebook.com/groups/imcircle/

This is a space that creates a virtual version of a men's circle where any man can share his challenges, life lessons and ask for advice, or simply be seen and heard.

LIFESTYLE DESIGN

Many years ago I came across the work of Dr John Demartini who taught me the importance of "Masterplanning" our lives. Tim Ferriss, in his book *The Four Hour Work Week,* calls this process "Lifestyle Design".

What I've noticed is that a small handful of people actively design the lives they want to live in detail and taking into account all the different areas of life.

Most people simply follow the path of least resistance. They follow the groove created by their emotional baggage and by the circumstances of their life. They never really sit back and ask:

Where am I headed?
Do I want this?
What else do I want?
What areas would I have to develop myself in if I want that?
Who can I learn from?

As a result most people live mediocre lives. They have a few areas where they experience comfort or happiness but largely their dreams go unlived and their potential is never experienced.

The challenge with this is, when we step outside the pathways that we are conditioned for we tend to face HUGE resistance. This is what happens when an employee decides to start their own business, or someone with strong religious conditioning decides to explore their sexuality, or a "mummy's boy" decides to take up boxing.

The new challenge pushes all of our buttons and reveals all of our hidden weaknesses–it's MUCH easier to go back to what we know... but for those of us who are prepared to develop our weaker aspects as well as our natural gifts, the depth of fulfillment and the impact we'll create in the long run is exponentially greater!

The following is a simple template I use to look over my life, using 7 main areas to help me reflect on all the different parts of myself. Looking at these areas will also inform which archetypes we want to work with later on.

THE MAIN AREAS OF LIFE:

Physical Health, Body and Well-being

This covers everything to do with our physical body and health. How do we want to eat, sleep, and how fit do we want to be? Are there health issues that need addressing? Do we have goals that relate to strength, fitness, physical capability or appearance?

Social Life and Recreation

This is about who I'm surrounded by socially and what I do for fun and entertainment. Remembering that the people I surround myself with shape who I become, I use this section to create a blueprint for the sort of friends, allies, mentors and teachers I want to attract into my life.

Money, Finances & Wealth

This is one of the areas that many people shy away from thinking about the most. When we have a clear vision for how much money we want to make, how we want to live, how we'd like to grow our wealth over time, and what we want to spend and invest it on, we take control of our financial future. This has a hugely empowering effect on all the other areas.

Love & Family Life

I divide this into two main areas: Romantic love and Family love.

Basically, how do I want my love/sex/dating life to look? With who do I spend it? What do we do? How do we relate to each other?

And then, how do I relate to my existing family? How often do we see each other etc.?

Career & Vocation

We live in a reality where–thanks to the internet– we can make a living doing literally ANYTHING we want. Yet, so many people work a job they hate and dedicate half of their life to something that has little or no meaning to them! When we take time to design clearly what we do for a living and for a creative outlet, over time we are able to move more and more into work that truly fulfills us and provides meaning to our lives.

Learning & Skill Development

"If you're not green and growing, you're ripe and rotten!" This is something one of my first mentors used to say over and over. In this area I have a shopping list of things I want to know about and things I want to get good at. This can range from practical skills (like how to do a handstand or how to shoot Facebook videos), to learning about subjects that interest me like ancient Egyptian history or reading about Bitcoin. It doesn't really matter. Just get clear on all the ways in which you want to continue to learn and grow!

Spirituality & Life Purpose

What's the point of life for you? What feelings do you like to experience that bring meaning and connection into your life? Some people are religious and some (me, for example) aren't. But... we all have certain things we do that make us feel more connected and alive (meditation, for example) and we all have things that bring purpose into our lives. You might not know the answers to this stuff but the point really is to start asking the questions.

Questions like:

What do I believe to be the purpose of my life?
What activities bring me into connection and stillness?
What activities are "spiritual" for me?

As I work through the different areas of life I break each one down into 3 sub-categories:

Being, Doing and Having.

This is a personal development model that helps us look at 3 areas; identity, behavior and results.

So if I mapped out my vision for Physical Health & Well-being it would look something like this:

PHYSICAL BODY:

BE: The healthiest, strongest version of myself.

DO: Eating 3 balanced meals daily. Lifting weights 4 times per week. Training Brazilian Jiujitsu 5 days a week. Stretching, yoga and foam roller each day. Get Massage. Get 7 to 8 hours sleep each night.

HAVE: Ability to deadlift 160kg. Visible abs/look good with shirt off. BJJ Blue Belt. Feeling well-rested and super strong.

For more help with Lifestyle design, watch the video and download the template HERE.

SOME TYPES OF INITIATION:

-Parting ways from our family.
-Facing physical hardships.
-Learning a difficult skill and being tested.
-Going into an altered state.
-Facing a fear.

QUIZ:

Surveying your life–list any events that have happened that you still haven't resolved. In other words things that happened, that when you remember them you still have bad feelings or wish they hadn't happened.

(only do the ages you've actually lived!)

From 0 to 7.
From 7 to 14.
From 14 to 21.
From 21 to 28.
From 28 to 35.
From 35 to 42.
From 42 to 49.
From 49 to 56.

After 56 to now.

List now what that event being unresolved has been costing you.

What are your top 5 fears?

List some ways you could face these.

THE ARCHETYPE CHALLENGE

"Who looks outside dreams, who looks inside awakes."
– Carl Jung

SECOND WARNING:

This is where shit is going to get a bit weird. Archetypes are powerful. During the seven-month archetype challenge I undertook during my research for this book in 2016, I often felt like I was possessed.

Once an archetype is "activated" it can seem to take on a life of its own. I write this not to discourage you from working with these energies–simply to give you a "heads up" of what you're getting into!

Please follow the instructions carefully if you decide to take on the challenge. This applies particularly to "opening" and "closing" the challenge so you have a clean sense of completion when you're done.

If you want to be guided on this journey, you can take my online integrated man archetype challenge–which is designed to accompany this book–here:

www.theintegratedman.com

BEFORE WORKING WITH ARCHETYPES:

So far we've looked at initiation and talked about developing new skills and facing dragons.

What I'm about to provide you with is a specific WAY to do this that doesn't require you to meet some mystical father figure or spend hundreds of dollars on workshops (although both of these can be valuable if you find the right ones!).

In a moment I'm going to introduce the different archetypes in detail and share some of my experiences working with them to give you the ideas and inspiration you need to create your own archetype challenge.

At the end of this chapter you'll find a quiz that can help you choose which archetypes to work with first.

I use this process to initiate myself all the time.

In other words, if I feel like I want to be more developed in an area of my life, I design a simple challenge for a set period of time (like a week or a month) and then I "step into" the right archetype to do the job.

The archetypes really can be thought of as "characters" that we step into or as software programs that we activate. This is far beyond "just pretending" though. In previous societies this sort of thing would be seen as an act of powerful ritual magic.

In our era it's more commonly seen as a way of working with our psychology and physiology to create a new result.

I see this as a really powerful way to:

1. Reveal my hidden weaknesses in an area of my character (facing dragons).
2. Develop new skills and abilities really, really quickly.

IN ORDER TO SUCCESSFULLY CONDUCT AN ARCHETYPE CHALLENGE

There are several things that need to happen in order to make this work smoothly.

We need to set our intentions clearly: In other words, choosing WHICH archetype you want to work with, setting an intention of why (getting clear on the outcome you want), and choosing a specific time period (e.g. 1 day, 1 week or 1 month).

For example:

"I'm going to work with "The Beast" for one month. I want to become stronger, more connected to my animal nature and more connected with the natural environment."

We need to choose activities and commit to them.

In order to create a change we need to immerse ourselves in thoughts and physically embodied feelings of the archetype we've chosen. For me, this looks like choosing one physical activity that I commit to every day and one mental or creative activity that sets a vibe too. I will also usually choose an object that represents the archetype as well.

Example:

"I'm going to lift weights and walk barefoot every day to bring the feelings of strength and grounded-ness into my life. I'm also going to listen to the Rewilding podcast to learn about hunter-gatherer societies and bush survival. I'm going to set up the Ram's skull and some bird wings on my altar in my bedroom."

We must keep a journal:

Journaling every day helps us notice what's going on. In the example above, all I'm really doing is lifting weights and learning about bush survival and putting a weird object in my room.

When you start journaling about the theme every day, something starts to happen... it really focuses our mind onto the subject and brings it deep into our life. It's not uncommon to start dreaming about the archetype and seeing it everywhere. This is where the change starts to happen.

We need to open and close the challenge properly.

This is REALLY important. The idea behind setting a fixed period of time is so that we know when the challenge starts and finishes. Mark the challenge on your calendar. On the day the challenge starts, set up your altar or pin up a picture representing the archetype you're going to work with. (I put a Ram's skull on my table but you could also put a picture of Wolverine or a wild animal on your wall.) At the end of the last day of the challenge, take the picture down.

I also say a simple opening statement on the first day and a simple closing statement on the last day.

EXAMPLE OF AN OPENING STATEMENT:

"I invite the beast archetype into my life and into my body."

EXAMPLE OF A CLOSING STATEMENT:

"I now declare this archetype experience closed."

Once the challenge is done, I recommend continuing to journal for another week to help make sense of it all. Usually after I've finished one of these challenges I like to ask myself, "What the fuck just happened!?"

It can also be helpful to have somewhere to share this experience. If you sign up for the archetype challenge online, we'll provide you with a group where you can share this with other people (who won't think you're going crazy).

If you aren't doing the online challenge, you can also share your experiences in the integrated men's circle online.

INTRODUCING THE INTEGRATED MAN ARCHETYPES

The following will provide you with a detailed introduction to the archetypes. The intention is that it will give you some inspiration and ideas for your own challenges. Pay attention to how you feel as you read about each one. Some will just "make sense". Others will seem confusing or even seem repulsive. This is a good indication that there's some work to do in this area.

NOTE ONE:

This is MY interpretation of these archetypes. Everyone is unique and as you go deeper with them you will find your own relationship to them. I've tried to share a mixture of what I've picked up from literature as well as my own experiences and my ultimate intention is that people work with these different aspects and make them their own.

NOTE TWO:

Don't worry if you feel like you're really undeveloped (or even completely fucked up) in one or more of these areas. The rating out of ten is a very loose scale also, you'll notice that I've been working with this stuff for years and still rate myself as a three out of ten in some areas. Don't let that discourage you. I'll provide a brief quiz at the end of the chapter to help you assess your strengths and weaknesses. Ultimately, the idea is to have fun with this stuff and to grow!

The beast

KEY TRAITS:

Body and earth connection. Wildness. Strength. Animalism. Rawness.

WHY THIS ENERGY IS IMPORTANT:

The beast is our connection to the earth and to our bodies. He may seem primitive and raw to our civilized brains but he possesses deep wisdom, knowledge and revitalizing power.

MY IMPRESSIONS OF THIS ARCHETYPE:

I first experienced this energy after injecting MDMA at a house party when I was eighteen. (I was a bit wild as a kid!)

As the lightening cracked in the background, something quickened inside me and I felt a dormant part of me awaken in a way I'd never before experienced. I stepped outside for a minute and the storm was torrential.

I ran through the storm shirtless–fat, warm, tropical raindrops splashing my skin. I could smell the moist earth and the lightning and my body was alive. I crouched beneath the partial shelter of a tree branch watching the downpour intently. No thoughts went through my head–I just WAS. I could feel my belly filling and emptying with my breath. I could feel my bare feet in the wet earth. I felt aroused in every sense of the word. I felt like I was part wolf, like I'd broken the chains of so-called civilization. Predatory energy washed through my body. I felt the OK-ness of my base desires to fuck, fight, scream in rage, jump and run and express the power of my physical body.

I was alive.

THE UNDERACTIVE EXPRESSION OF THE BEAST:

Since the advent of Christianity (and any other religion that preaches that the body is somehow dirty or sinful), most of society has learned to suppress our bodily expression and/or animalistic nature.

It's easy to recognize when someone is uncomfortable around this energy.

They will be awkward when references to sexuality come up, have body image issues, be disgusted by regular bodily functions and smells and not be particularly connected to nature.

They will be very "in their heads" and probably won't know what they are feeling physically or emotionally at any given time.

Collectively, we could regard the destruction of our natural habitat as directly caused by our disconnection from this energy.

THE OVERACTIVE EXPRESSION OF THE BEAST:

When the beast is overactive we are subject to the whims of the body. For most people this will only happen if we are intoxicated or strongly triggered, but for some people impulse control has never been developed. Whatever the cause, overactive expression of the beast can manifest in violence, inappropriate animalistic behavior, rape, and uncontrollable physical expressions such as howling, screaming, trembling etc.

THE INTEGRATED EXPRESSION OF THE BEAST:

When this energy is integrated and active we have effortless access to our body's deep wisdom. We are connected to the natural environment. Our natural response to strong emotions is to shake, to make sound and to move the excess energy through the body. We feel safe in our physical body; we feel no shame in its shape, its appearance its sounds or its smells. We are neither obsessed by nor in denial of sexuality. We are connected to our physicality but not ruled by it. Healthy connection to this energy will usually result in robust physical health and comfort with the natural environment.

WHAT I DID IN MY CHALLENGE:

I committed to working largely on my physical body and also connecting with nature more. I lifted heavy weights 4 days a week, ate 3 meat meals a day and went swimming in the lake and slept on the beach. I also set up an altar in my garden with a Ram's skull and a pile of weightlifting plates to symbolize my connection to my physical body.

WHAT HAPPENED:

I felt heavy and ashamed and realized I still have some hatred of, and disconnection from, my body. I had a fight with my partner that escalated almost into domestic violence that came seemingly out of nowhere. I had very low energy for other tasks such as working on my business or socializing. I got bigger and stronger over this month.

WHAT I LEARNED:

That there was a lot of suppressed rage in my body. Also that I'm not that connected to nature–I felt afraid swimming in the lake in the early morning and I have lots of childhood trauma around being weak or sick that has to be faced as I get bigger and stronger.

In relation to the fight I had with Vanessa, I learned that because of my lack of physical connection I've let myself be pushed around emotionally for most of my life. Luckily, we didn't seriously hurt each other but I got a deep insight into how domestic violence emerges from men not having the presence to witness their emotions of rage or hurt AND from men not being aware that they are carrying emotional wounds.

This was an intense and eye-opening few weeks. I'm grateful that it wasn't worse and it gave me a really strong reminder to be mindful of going into these archetypes!

ACTIVITIES:
Weightlifting. Self-pleasure. Eating meat. Sleeping in nature. Being in nature. Massage. Connecting to the body. Brazilian Jiujitsu. Animal movements.

OBJECTS:
Ram's skull. Weights. Sticks and leaves and dirt.

MEDIA:
Watched *Wolverine.* (I guess that's overactive beast!)
Listened to the Rewilding podcast.
Read *Iron John,* Robert Bly's book about "the wild man".

DANE'S STOCKTAKE
I would say this energy started as a 1/10 for me.
I finished at about a 3/10.
This is clearly my most fucked up archetype.

The lover

KEY TRAITS:

Sensuality. Pleasure. Seduction. Connection. Creativity. Intimacy

WHY THIS ENERGY IS IMPORTANT:

The lover is the giver of appreciation and the gateway to pleasure and play. He is the channel through which the masculine can appreciate, connect and enjoy.

MY IMPRESSIONS OF THIS ARCHETYPE:

Back in 2011, I had my first lingham (Sanskrit word for cock–literally meaning "wand of light") massage. I didn't really know what to expect. I sat with the practitioner before the session and we discussed what I wanted to get from it. "I want to be more in my masculine!" I'd been working on presence, power, purpose for the last 3 years and something STILL wasn't working in my life. I figured I needed to be "more masculine". She smiled and said, "I think you might be OK there; what about your softer side?" I instantly felt really nervous. Hmmm. OK, I think you might be right. We sat and eye gazed for a few minutes to create a sense of connection. It was the first time I'd experienced this, it felt weird and vulnerable but also nice. I was scared yet aroused and "nothing had happened yet".

Eventually I lay down naked and she gave me an intimate, erotic, full body massage. She encouraged me to make sounds and breathe, which back then was quite unfamiliar. I noticed that when I did that I felt a LOT of emotion, sexual excitement, deep sadness, even anger and rage.

Deep in the session she began working on my abdomen and stimulating my cock. The energy from my cock would wash through my whole body and seemed to highlight a really tight part in my belly. "Go into it," she told me. I felt into the area and instantly felt pain and anger. A memory I didn't really understand, from early childhood I guess, washed through. It was something about being replaced or not being important or not being loved. I screamed really loud and the tears began to flow. Straight after that, orgasmic energy began to flow. I had a non-ejaculatory orgasm – big waves of energy washing through my body over and over. I realized on some level that my ability to experience pleasure and my ability to experience painful emotion were inextricably linked. I was never the same again after that experience. It's like my feeling body had been reconnected to my heart and brain.

During sex I could FEEL everything about my partner. I would often know what was going on inside her better than she did. I became less rigid. More OK with moving my hips and making sounds when I felt trapped emotions in my body. That first session was a significant initiation into "The Lover".

THE UNDERACTIVE EXPRESSION OF THE LOVER:

When a man has no connection to his lover energy, he is dry and rigid.

He will be embarrassed or awkward about intimacy and sensitivity. He will be completely disconnected from his own femininity and sweetness and will externally project it onto women. He will derive his worth from work and "doing things" and struggle to enjoy sensory pleasures. In truth, he is afraid of being vulnerable. He may regard men who are fluent in this energy as "weak" or "gay" or untrustworthy.

THE OVERACTIVE EXPRESSION OF THE LOVER:

The other side of the coin is the man who can happily lounge around all day, everyday having sex and eating strawberries and listening to music and flowing. The enjoyment of pleasure has become an addiction–something he uses to validate himself but also to avoid the world.

Overactive lover energy will make a man indecisive and he will tend to shy away from anything that causes discomfort or requires discipline and focus.

THE INTEGRATED EXPRESSION OF THE LOVER:

A man who is integrated in this energy has a nice balance of structure and flow. He can be charming and seductive and drop deeply into pleasure and emotion but he doesn't DROWN there. He still holds structure and direction, just not rigidly.

WHAT I DID IN MY CHALLENGE:

I dedicated several weeks to learning yoni (the Sanskrit work for pussy meaning 'source') massage under the tutelage of a skilled female practitioner and saw clients regularly. I wrote poetry and went to 5 RHYTHMS dance and took some salsa classes and did some tantra workshops. I journaled my sexual fantasies and watched romance movies and erotic films.

WHAT HAPPENED:

I felt a deep appreciation of women coming through in my life. Some of the yoni massage sessions were profoundly heart-opening and arousing. I began reflecting on my relationship and felt a strong desire to be freer to flirt and play with different lovers. I began to think that maybe I'm not meant to be monogamous. This brought up a lot of turmoil inside me in relation to my relationship and the agreements within it.

WHAT I LEARNED:

That this part of me is quite strong. I'm very emotional and sensitive. I love the company of women so much. Also, I realized that many of my assumptions about how relationship SHOULD be have been based on my upbringing. There are still some blocks in this area; some guilt and fear about what would happen if I truly just dived into my lover identity.

ACTIVITIES:
Dance. Self-pleasure. Erotic massage. Flirting.

OBJECTS:
I put a candle in the shape of two lovers on my altar. Also a collection of colorful stones.

MEDIA:
I watched *Vicky Cristina Barcelona.*
Read tantra books and books about relationships.
Love Freedom and Aloneness - Osho
Wired for Love - Stan Tatkin
The Course of Love - Alain de Botton

DANE'S STOCKTAKE:
At the beginning – 4/10
By the end – 7/10

The warrior

KEY TRAITS:

Focus. Determination. Facing death. Life direction. Discipline. Honesty.

WHY THIS ENERGY IS IMPORTANT:

Without the warrior, nothing gets done. This energy is the epitome of masculine drive and action. It's also the ability to cut through bullshit and get to the truth. The warrior sets standards, commits, never gives up and protects the kingdom at all costs.

MY IMPRESSIONS OF THIS ARCHETYPE:

My initiation into the warrior was a less conscious one than many of the others. I'd been bullied in high school for three years. I was like a cross between a science geek and a white gangster rapper that hadn't quite figured out how to integrate the two sides. The football-playing alpha male kids at my school didn't like me and for some reason I would always challenge them back whenever they spoke to me.

One night at a school dance, I got jumped in the carpark by one of the guys who was a football player and a decent boxer. He tapped me on the shoulder and as I turned around he punched me in the face. What he didn't know was that I was carrying a knife. I showed it to him in the expectation it would scare him away. He told me to "drop it or I'll smash you". When he took the next swing I stabbed him in the chest.

That moment changed my life in a thousand ways. I moved from terror to fury in a split second. He did the same thing but in the opposite direction. He was bleeding from the chest and arm and trying pathetically to crawl away from me as I screamed at him.

The awkward, nerdy kid had just destroyed the school bully. Kids gathered around. I handed over the knife. One parent berated me and told me, "Real men fight with their fists." The police were called and eventually came and took me away.

I was charged with attempted murder and eventually plead guilty to the lesser charge of unlawful wounding. I faced many difficult months after that incident and watched my family crack under the pressure in many ways. It was a tough time but I am very grateful for it.

Now, years later, I've trained myself in more resourceful ways to access the warrior but I remain grateful for the first time he broke through and transformed my life.

I killed a dragon that night. I would never again be a victim or believe that any situation could not be overcome. On the other hand, I anchored some pretty negative stuff to the expression of warrior – for a long time it was synonymous with hurting others and breaking laws. I would eventually come to regard that as the dis-integrated version of it.

THE UNDERACTIVE EXPRESSION OF THE WARRIOR:

When you meet a man who's really lacking in this energy, you might want to slap him. He's probably gentle and kind but will lack the ability to take decisive action. A huge amount of what our culture calls "being a man" is really the warrior archetype. When this is absent or suppressed (often because of negative and painful associations to the destruction that this energy can cause when it's overactive), the result is a guy who can't "get his shit together", who lets the world pass him by and struggles to act.

THE OVERACTIVE EXPRESSION OF THE WARRIOR:

The other end of the spectrum is very common in our society. Men who take action without thinking, for whom everything is a competition or a challenge, and work is life. The overactive warrior is ALWAYS at war, ALWAYS on a mission. He's not receptive, he has no time to feel his feelings and he will struggle with intimacy or vulnerability. The primary focus will be on "winning" and competition.

THE INTEGRATED EXPRESSION OF THE WARRIOR:

When this energy is in balance it provides a strong ability to execute and get stuff done as well as the confidence to name awkward situations and cut through the bullshit WITH SENSITIVITY. The integrated warrior is in sync with the seasonal nature of life, he's not attempting to always be "on". He embraces the hard and the soft and the active and passive stages of a project. The integrated warrior is not afraid of feeling but is also capable of sometimes putting emotion aside and handling the task at hand.

WHAT I DID IN MY CHALLENGE:

I set a goal to get really good at Brazilian Jiujitsu and also to reassess my life and get honest with myself about who I am and where I'm headed.

WHAT HAPPENED:

The Jiujitsu part didn't really take off. I trained a little but actually what came up here was a lot of stuff around the idea that I'm not living up to the standards I want to in my life.

WHAT I LEARNED:

A lot came up around money and business and I realized I've been taking it easy and playing safe in many areas. I also realized that I really struggle to set boundaries with people, both in my relationships and friendships but with clients as well.

I realized that the warrior doesn't have to be literal. I kept thinking about my childhood and all the fights I got into and it seems that really a lot of it was about standards and boundaries.

I worked through Tony Robbins' *Awaken the Giant Within* and really reset the standards I want in my life; for my body, my money, my relationships and my business, and I also decided to start fixing up my back taxes!

ACTIVITIES:
Goal-setting. Life assessment. Having tough conversations. Reflecting on conflict in my life.
I was given the question:
"What does Dane want?"

OBJECTS:
Martial arts belt.
A knife (symbolizing cutting through bullshit).
Obsidian stone (self reflections).

MEDIA:

I watched a lot of fantasy movies and really got the realization that a lot of bullshit surrounds the warrior ideal in our society.

DANE'S STOCKTAKE

Started 5/10 but with some wounding around boundaries.
Finished 6/10 and with a deeper understanding.

The king

KEY TRAITS:

Fairness. Integrity. Prosperity. Organization. Gratitude. Sovereignty.

WHY THIS ENERGY IS IMPORTANT:

The king is both the father of the kingdom and the central principle around which it is organized. He brings structure, justice, fairness, integrity and balance to everything he touches. Without the King, there is no safety and no integrity.

MY IMPRESSIONS OF THIS ARCHETYPE:

I remember the first time I met a man who held a strong KING energy. He was the manager of sales operation for which I worked as a trainer. He was a large guy who seemed completely unconcerned by what anyone thought of him. He was measured and certain in his actions and instructions, and yet he would listen to those around him carefully and weigh what they had to say. He was strong but not overbearing. Clear and direct but not rude. He cared about other people but would not bend his rules or principles to accommodate them.

What I noticed was that when he was present, everything seemed to fall into a state of order and organization. He didn't really DO anything to make it happen, it was simply his way of being. When he showed up, everything and everyone would organize themselves around him, and we knew if we did that we'd be safe and we'd prosper.

THE UNDERACTIVE EXPRESSION OF THE KING:

Our current society does not honor the king energy much. The father character in most TV shows is a bumbling fool, our governments are corrupt and the word "patriarchy" is the most derogatory one in the entire feminist lexicon. We live in an era where kings are rare.

A man who does not have access to the king firstly is disorganized and lacks in self-worth and value. This may show up materially or it may be in his bearing. The king takes the longest to master of all the archetypes (since it requires the ability to balance all the others), so it's normal that younger men don't have much king energy.

Lack of king energy can show up as impatience, instability, and a lack of ability to just BE. It also is indicated by a man who doesn't know his moral code or his purpose OR who will easily compromise his values for the approval of others.

THE OVERACTIVE EXPRESSION OF THE KING:

The overactive king is "the tyrant". This energy is a sort of bullying control-freak. It usually conceals a lack of control or self-worth that is being covered up by becoming overbearing, like a lizard or a toad that swells itself up to ward off threats!

THE INTEGRATED EXPRESSION OF THE KING :

When the king is integrated, well, it's a wonderful thing. The king archetype is the central archetype, just as the heart is the central chakra. The king is the expression of divine order in the material realm. He is the masculine, nurturing principle that maintains healthy boundaries, repairs broken relationships, cultivates prosperity and lives a life in service of the grand, organized design.

In order for the king archetype to be strong and balanced, a man must be able to "think from his heart", to be able to create order and calmness in the centre of his mind, to love without fear, to act decisively and to dedicate his life to the building of a legacy far greater than his own.

This tends to take a lot longer to develop than the other archetypes, chiefly because maturity is one of its characteristics. Also because the king is able to draw on the other archetypes and moderate them so... if we don't have a healthy warrior or a healthy connection to the magician, our king will be in some way imbalanced or lacking. In many ways the king is a healthy, stable, integrated man.

WHAT I DID IN MY CHALLENGE:

I revisited my moral code. I spent time with older men (notably one guy who is the CEO of a successful company). I brought more integrity into my business systems and I reflected on my ideas around family.

WHAT HAPPENED:

I can't believe that two weeks ago I wanted to fuck everyone. As soon as this energy kicked in I wanted to become a father. On the second night in king, I watched *The Lion King* and cried for about half an hour. I wrote a long journal entry about the sort of relationship I want to experience and the sort of family life I want. I also spent time with a guy I respect who is quite wealthy and got to know him a little more.

WHAT I LEARNED:

That the king is skilled in diplomacy (I learned this talking about business with the CEO). He was so much more patient than me in how he resolved issues among his leadership team. I saw why I only had one staff member –I'm very impatient and intolerant AND I realized how much more nurturing I need to bring in to my life if I want to, A) have a successful business, let alone, B) raise a family.

I also learned that the king and the father are directly linked and that a huge amount of my distrust in authority is really a mirror of my own lack of self-trust in my masculine leadership.

ACTIVITIES:
Fatherhood movies. Being mentored by older men. Healing family wounds.

OBJECTS:
I literally put a crown and a golden dollar sign necklace on my altar, as well as a picture of my family.

MEDIA:
The Lion King.
Lord of the Rings.

DANE'S STOCKTAKE:
This is a really big one for me.
Before – 4/10.
After – 5/10.

The poet

KEY TRAITS:

Creative expression, inspiration, intuition, mystery, leadership.

WHY THIS ENERGY IS IMPORTANT:

The poet is our ability to voice the truth to speak from the heart; to express our finer emotions such as gratitude, devotion, love and vulnerability, and to lead and inspire others by doing so.

MY IMPRESSIONS OF THIS ARCHETYPE:

The first time I ever stepped on stage with no plan, the poet was with me. He is the act of trusting in pure creativity. He is present when a wrong note becomes part of a new song. When an idea comes to you in your sleep the poet is present. He is inspiration incarnate. When the words speak you, when the dance dances you, when you play guitar and you forget that you're playing–when life flows through you and the mind simply watches, the poet is with you.

THE UNDERACTIVE EXPRESSION OF THE POET:

In so many industries the act of copying other people's ideas is the norm. TV shows, advertising campaigns, even in the world of music and books and in the workshop scene, most people simply copy other people's ideas. The underactive poet is more common than not. A lack of originality and deep creative expression is the norm in today's world. People are content to communicate in small talk, regurgitating old social scripts and expressing themselves without any depth whatsoever.

THE OVERACTIVE EXPRESSION OF THE POET:

The overactive poet is less common but does exist. It's that guy who's ideas are truly brilliant but who drowns you in a torrent of his own genius He doesn't care if you have ideas too, he won't pause long enough to find out. The overactive poet is not at all receptive and is fueled by a lack of expression in daily life. The person who should have written books or been a speaker or artist but who has not followed their path will be forced to expel this energy by talking you to death.

THE INTEGRATED EXPRESSION OF THE POET:

When the poet is integrated we have a man who speaks clearly and powerfully (or whose art or work speaks for him). This person is able to listen and doesn't need to prove his genius because that genius is fully expressed in the world. The business is built, the songs are written, the movies are made. Ironically, the integrated poet doesn't need to tell you what an amazing leader he is–he's busy inspiring and leading.

WHAT I DID IN MY CHALLENGE:

I committed to write poetry, journal and shoot videos every day.

WHAT HAPPENED:

I didn't want to. There was huge resistance. I ran an event in Melbourne and housesat a friend's house. The event went well, although the house was cold and I felt miserable the whole time. Eventually, on a whim, I rented a 5-star hotel room with a view of the whole city. It felt amazing. I let myself off the hook from writing poetry and enjoyed my hotel room. I bought some new clothes and got a lingham massage. I went home and after three weeks away from training I entered my first BJJ competition and won gold!

WHAT I LEARNED:

Again, the poet is not such a literal expression. I didn't feel the urge to write poetry– in fact, I uncovered (much like the beast) the realization that I have a lot of wounds in relation to my creativity. Big issues around being seen and stories about competing with others. What I did realize is that my business, the workshops I run, my clothing, my sexuality and even martial arts are all forms of expression of who I am. The integrated man, the person I am becoming, is my true work of art and so is my business.

ACTIVITIES:

Teaching others, enjoying refinement and nice things, business, movement, sex, spiritual practice.

OBJECTS:

I couldn't find any objects that represented the poet to me!

MEDIA:

I read the books *The War of Art by Stephen Pressfield* and *Good to Great* by Jim Collins

DANE'S STOCKTAKE:

Before I started this was literally 0/10.
When I finished – 3/10.

The magician

KEY TRAITS:

Systems thinking. Vision. Insight. Transformation.

WHY THIS ENERGY IS IMPORTANT:

The magician plays the role of advisor. He is the one who sees beyond the realm of the physical to the causal level. The magician doesn't take a lot of action, he makes things happen through timing, leverage and the magic of ideas and words. The magician is the gateway to an awakened mind and a mastery of secret knowledge.

The Magician is a master manifester and utilizes intellect, visionary capacity, intuition and conscious intention to create the world around him. He understands that all is not what it seems and that the seen world is simply an EFFECT of the unseen world.

He realizes that the "rules of the game" are hidden beneath the surface and that many of the principles that lead to mastery of the various areas of life are counter-intuitive.

A good magician knows what to learn, how to internalize it quickly and how to leverage that knowledge powerfully to create transformation.

Magic can be used to create change in the external world OR to integrate and evolve the inner self in order to connect with the Tao, the universe or God.

MY IMPRESSIONS OF THIS ARCHETYPE:

The magician archetype is the one I've played in the most and the most literally. One night before I was going away for the weekend I performed a simple sigil magick ritual. Sigil magick is where you write down an intention or affirmation, turn the statement into a symbol and then "charge" that symbol with your energy and intention.

This one simply said, "I want a nice new apartment with good carpets". I performed the process, packed my bag and then went away to a meditation retreat.

Ten days later I emerged from the retreat and switched on my phone. The first text said, "Your apartment has been flooded, please contact us." I called the number and the landlords told me that a water heater had exploded, flooding the house and destroying the carpet, and that it would need to be re-carpeted and repainted. I stayed in a hotel for a week and when I returned home I literally had "a nice new apartment with good carpets".

I made a note to myself to be careful what I ask for.

THE UNDERACTIVE EXPRESSION OF THE MAGICIAN:

The mentally unawake person is lacking in magician energy. They take things on face value and believe what they are told. They're are easily manipulated and cannot see the bigger picture; life for them is just one day after another with no plan and no vision.

THE OVERACTIVE EXPRESSION OF THE MAGICIAN

The overactive magician lives in his head. He is manipulative and deceitful and lost in his own imagination and fears. It's very hard to take action from this place because the complexity of the mind seduces and imprisons him. The overactive magician often THINKS that he is powerful but is incapable of taking action in the physical world.

THE INTEGRATED EXPRESSION OF THE MAGICIAN:

When the magician is integrated, strategy and big picture thinking meets action. It is as though the magician has become the advisor and the other archetypes are each empowered to play their part working toward the greater vision that the magician can see.

WHAT I DID IN MY CHALLENGE:

Visioning. Ritual. Life design. Running workshops.

WHAT HAPPENED:

Crazy mixture of power and insecurities. Had a wild phone sex connection with a woman I've never met. Ran 2 Spiral experiences. Got into some kinky BDSM dynamics and playing with power. Noticing that women are attracted to me when I'm in this energy.

WHAT I LEARNED:

Wow. What a crazy month. Magician is definitely my strongest one but it's also got wounds and crazy stuff in there. I guess it goes back to being a nerd in school. Lots of fears about women not being attracted to me alternating with women coming out of the woodwork and having sexual experiences with me. It's very easy for me to get stuck in my mind visualizing my life over and over again–the journals for this one read very intense and crazy!

ACTIVITIES:
Rituals. Tantric sex. Life design.

OBJECTS:
So many objects; magic box,
obsidian rings and quartz crystals.

MEDIA:
Watched lots of magick movies.

DANE'S STOCKTAKE
Before – 7/10 (lots of weird stuff in there!).
After – 9/10 but also healthier.

The god

KEY TRAITS:

Oneness. Stillness. Pure presence. Surrender. Witness consciousness.

WHY THIS ENERGY IS IMPORTANT:

The God represents the transcendence of polarity. The God is the pure consciousness that sits beyond light or dark, masculine or feminine, hard or soft, physical or mental.

Beneath the ever-changing moods and emotional weather of the ego resides a stillness and a state of BEING-NESS that is unchangeable, imperturbable and immortal.

From this place there is no desire, no earthly concerns, no concept of loss or gain, good or bad–there just IS.

MY IMPRESSIONS OF THIS ARCHETYPE:

I remember the first time I dropped into pure witness consciousness. There was no thoughts, no one home... yet, I (or some version of "I") was still watching in the background.

It was in the middle of a transfiguration (eye gazing) ritual and the small "I" was just completely gone. It wasn't dramatic, I wasn't in an altered state, I could just simply see that the person in front of me was me and I was them and there was no difference or separation between us. I could see that the idea of "objects" was an illusion. There just IS.

THE UNDERACTIVE EXPRESSION OF THE GOD:

Life is so serious. Every problem is a drama. It's like it never occurred to them that we're all just piles of atoms whizzing around and we're all going to die soon enough. This is the lower level of the human condition – again, taking life at face value and being completely identified with the self and the problems of everyday life as though they are utterly and completely real.

THE OVERACTIVE EXPRESSION OF THE GOD:

When this energy is overactive the person is hardly here. There's no acknowledgment of the human existence or good or bad. Everything just is. This, when not embodied, is the epitome of spiritual bypassing. This is the person who never admits to having a bad day or acknowledging the basic realities of life. They are lost in the high of the white light!

THE INTEGRATED EXPRESSION OF THE GOD:

When we can be in the world, but not completely of it, we're experiencing an integrated expression of the God energy. When we can zoom out and see that it's all ultimately meaningless but then still engage heart and soul with the day-to-day of being a human being. When we can periodically allow ourselves to drop into stillness and remember that all the content of our minds is just that–content. Then life becomes an enjoyable game.

WHAT I DID IN MY CHALLENGE:

Delivering consciousness-raising events. Started a daily zen meditation practice. Rest after this whole journey and being on tour for several weeks.

WHAT HAPPENED:

I got more space around my interactions with women and my stories around relationships.

I was able to witness myself more and get out of my thoughts. I had a movement retreat booked in but I cancelled it at the last minute.

WHAT I LEARNED:

My whole life is crazy. The less I try to DO the more powerful it seems I am in the world. It's like my ego is trying SO hard all the time and actually the more I just sit back and LET things happen, the more powerful it all is.

ACTIVITIES:

Zen meditation. Being. Movement practice. Sex.

OBJECTS:

None.

MEDIA:
Listening to Eckart Tolle's *The Power of Now.*

DANE'S STOCKTAKE:
Before – 4/10.
After – 6/10.

The inner child

I finished my archetype challenge and after all the highs and lows and learnings about the seven archetypes, something felt unfinished. A couple of times I'd find myself in sexual situations unable to "perform". Something was off. When I would journal I got this sense that my "little boy" was terrified. A fear would rise up inside me and I'd freeze. It seemed especially common during moments of sexual connection when it was getting heated. I realized that it was my inner child–the message seemed to be, "I'm scared you'll abandon me." This was either a new thing or something I got so used to ignoring that I'd never noticed it before. I got a sense that it was BIG and an important addition to the integrated man journey. I realized that this unmet child was having a huge impact on my relationships–I wouldn't be capable of mature relationship until I built a connection with him and he trusted me…

KEY TRAITS:

Innocence. Security. Trust. Pure emotion. Sensitivity. Vulnerability. Joy. Wonder.

WHY THIS ENERGY IS IMPORTANT:

Without this being healthy there is NO way to access the man in a clean way. If the inner child is unhappy ALL of the adult energies will show up in a distorted fashion. This is why we have many powerful but fundamentally immature men running the world at the current time. When we can actually feel and nourish the inner child, the king comes into balance and is able to hold space for others. Until we can hold space for the most vulnerable part of ourself, however, the state of sovereignty created by the king will be fragile.

MY IMPRESSIONS OF THIS ARCHETYPE:

We were on the verge of breaking up, for what felt like the hundredth time. This time she seemed fine with it. I named, "I'm out. I love you so much but I don't feel like I can be 100% IN with anyone until I've explored more parts of myself."

Up until now I'd been terrified that saying this would hurt her, but this time, she responded in a really measured and confident way. "I understand." As soon as she said it I started freaking out. What had I done? I was going to be alone! This fear wasn't coming from my adult self–it was coming from him, my little boy.

Vanessa seemed to know what was going on, she held me energetically and started talking me through a process. She got me to draw a picture of my inner child and how he felt–it was an angry red ball with a face. It looked like a four year old had drawn it. Then she told me to write all the qualities that I was dependent on the relationship for. I wrote them. Happiness, safety, joy, fun etc. Then I cried like I've hardly ever cried in my life. I drew more and more pictures, all in this child-like style. I drew what he needed (a picture of a tree house and pictures of lizards and waterfalls) and then I drew his future–a picture of me and him going on adventures.

I thought I'd finished the adventure but I realized–I had one more archetype to work with AND it was by far the most important one of them all–it was my inner child.

THE UNDERACTIVE EXPRESSION OF THE INNER CHILD:

Without this part being connected, a man is full of bravado. He can't actually feel his own fear. There's a disconnect. I suspect that most men are in this state. Occasionally the unheard inner child will cease the reigns, maybe the adult man will freeze during a business deal or while fucking his wife (erectile dysfunction is often this energy coming through), or experience anxiety or paranoia–all symptoms of the unheard inner child trying to get attention.

THE OVERACTIVE EXPRESSION OF THE INNER CHILD:

This is most common in the early stages of making connection to this part of ourselves. Unconsolable crying, fear of isolation and sensations of helplessness, needing women to mother us or speaking in baby voices are all overactive expressions of the inner child (as usually this is typically caused in response to the underactive expression).

THE INTEGRATED EXPRESSION OF THE INNER CHILD:

When the inner child is integrated, many of the traits of mature, stable masculinity will be present. The man is able to be simultaneously strong and sensitive. He can FEEL himself and feel his lover without being overwhelmed. He's able to hold space for a partner because he's holding space for himself. He also knows his own boundaries well–he's neither reckless with intimacy or aloof and avoidant. He can sit stable in the field of love and intimacy.

WHAT I DID IN MY CHALLENGE

I booked a treehouse in the mountains for 3 weeks to journal and meditate on my journey so far and practice self-care and self-love.

WHAT HAPPENED:

I mostly stayed in the cabin, climbed in the mountains and journaled. I meditated every day and spent time lying with my hands on my body, loving myself. I also had a lot of mother-child wounds heal. Interestingly, I had drawn lizards and spiders on my child-like drawing and I had numerous visits from lizards and spiders, including a small goanna that broke into my house and a giant goanna (like 8 feet long) that ran into the bush.

WHAT I LEARNED:

That wounded inner child stuff had been running my life, especially my intimate relationships up until this point. That the need to "plug in" to women to get nurturance and love is a form of dependency that causes codependence in relationship. By the end of the 3 weeks I began to feel that I was able to give myself all the qualities on my list that previously I had only been able to source from my relationship.

ACTIVITIES:

Things I loved as a kid. Nurturing activities. Cooking for myself. Abstaining from contact with women I had attractions or intimate connection with. Climbing trees. Playing in the river. Writing. Drawing. Singing. Making fire.

OBJECTS:

Inner child drawing.

MEDIA:
I scanned a few books on child psychology for ideas and watched comic book movies.

DANE'S STOCKTAKE
This was 0/10 when I began.
It was 5/10 by the end.

That gives you a brief introduction to the eight Masculine Archetypes I work with in the Integrated Man Project.

From here it's up to you with regards to what you would like to DO with that information!

My recommendation is that you create a simple challenge for yourself to step into one of these archetypes and see what it has to teach you.

Maybe you instantly knew that there was one that really attracts you to work with OR maybe there's one that terrifies you or makes you feel uncomfortable and you know that's the one for you.

You can't really pick wrong. Even when I work with one that I'm really strong in (e.g. the Magician) all kinds of new lessons about myself come up!

If you want a little help deciding which one to start with, below is a simple question that can help you.

Which of the following areas of your life do you most want to empower?

My physical body & earth connection (beast).
My sex life and intimacy (lover).
My ability to kick arse and get shit done (warrior).
My masculine maturity (king).
My self-expression (poet).
My intelligence (magician).
My connection to the universe (god).
My sense of safety and innocence (inner child).

CLOSING WORDS:

If you made it this far – congratulations. My intention for this piece of writing is that it transmits to you some of what I've learned in my journey as a man so far. I'm far from perfect, just another human trying to make sense of it all BUT I have found huge wisdom and power in some of the pieces I've shared with you here.

When we understand that there are natural stages that we move through as men...

When we realize that we can take charge of our own development and the frames through which we see the world...

When we willingly step into challenges that will stretch us and cause us to face our dragons...

Then life becomes an empowering, exciting adventure filled with purpose, transformation and fulfillment.

This is what I wish for you and for everyone I come into contact with.

I invite you to find me online and to work with me in a closer capacity so we can lead a revolution in the world of awakened and complete manhood and masculinity.

Love,

Dane Tomas.

RESOURCES:

Archetype Activities Lists

Here are some of the activities I dedicated myself to for each one:

BEAST
Make wildman altar
Weightlifting
Nature connection
Nudity
Sleep outdoors
Detox/colonic
Foot & leg massage
Anal massage
Breathwork
Shaking
Re-sensitizing through movement/natural breath
Root chakra yoga postures
Animal movements
Shamanic initiation
DMT
Horse stance
Animalistic fucking

LOVER

Yoni massage
Contact improvisation
Lomi lomi/kahuna massage
Latin dance
BDSM/spanking
Polarity practice
New clothes/stylist
Hosting dinner party
Lingham massage
Approaching & complimenting women
Gourmet food tasting
Dancing eros/stripping
Abdominal massage

WARRIOR

MMA/muay thai/boxing
Pistol shooting
Horse stance
BJJ–competition on last day of warrior
Bow and arrow shooting
Qi Gong
Goal-setting
Running
Mountain climbing
Facing death
Haka
Tattoo
Warrior pose and solar plexus chakra yoga postures
Bodyweight exercise
Timed challenges e.g. burpees

KING

Hang out with my dad
Hanging out with the CEO of a company
Financial planning/wealth mindset study
Reassessing my moral code, integrity, boundaries and agreements
Leadership training
Gratitude practice
Clean up house & possessions
Ordering and systematizing
Legacy planning and long term life plans
Heart chakra asana

POET
Public speaking classes
Standup comedy
Freestyling daily
Posting daily videos on Facebook & Youtube
Reading (aloud) the best poets
Get an article published
Juggling
Improv
Acting
Storytelling
Singing/chanting
Going on the radio/TV/podcasts
Beatmaking/music recording

MAGICIAN

Learning–neuroscience, quantum physics, magical practice
Sigil magic
Ritual
Dream diary
Hypnosis practice
Vision boarding
Tarot/runes
Filmmaking
Horse whispering
Qi Gong
Reading high consciousness spiritual writings & texts
Vision quest
John Demartini
Brain health supplements
Concentration meditation

GOD

Retreat in nature
Silence
Meditation
Transfiguration
Purification/shanka cleanse/fasting
Kundalini yoga practice
Life purpose writing
Digital detox
Reading deep spiritual philosophy

INNER CHILD

Self nurturing
Drawing
Playing
Singing
Climbing trees
Playing with bugs and animals
Singing
Time separate from women
Staying in a treehouse
Making fire

USEFUL ORGANISATIONS & LINKS:

The Integrated Men's Circle Online:
https://www.facebook.com/groups/imcircle/

This is a place you can share your experiences in private with other men. It's also a great place to find out about more avenues for growth and development!

The Mankind Project:
http://mankindproject.org/

The ManKind Project is men's community for the 21st Century. MKP is a nonprofit training and education organization with three decades of proven success hosting life-changing experiential personal development programs for men. MKP supports a global network of free peer-facilitated men's groups.

ISTA–International School of Temple Arts
https://www.schooloftemplearts.org/

ISTA: International School of Temple Arts is committed to raising consciousness & sexuality education across the globe to grow community, provide conferences, events, and trainings to individuals, practitioners and teachers, and to provide business tools and collaborations to support the emergence of the Temple Arts around the world.

5 Rhythms

Gabrielle Roth's 5Rhythms® were continually inspired by her home base in New York City where she founded The Moving Center® in 1977. With over 400 certified teachers worldwide offering cutting edge core instruction through an ongoing curriculum of classes, workshops, and trainings–the 5Rhythms has grown to a global community born to dance, sweat, change, and support.

VIPASSANA:
https://www.dhamma.org/

The technique of Vipassana Meditation is taught at ten-day residential courses during which participants learn the basics of the method, and practise sufficiently to experience its beneficial results. There are no charges for the courses–not even to cover the cost of food and accommodation. All expenses are met by donations from people who, having completed a course and experienced the benefits of Vipassana, wish to give others the opportunity to also benefit.

Dancing Eros:
https://www.dancingeros.com

Dancing Eros explores and focuses on the authentic sexual and sensual embodiment of the five female erotic archetypes.

RECOMMENDED READING LIST:

Rubenstein, Arne. *The Making of Men*, 2013.

Deida, David. *The Way of the Superior Man*, 1997.

Bly, Robert. *Iron John: A Book About Men*, 1990.

Gillett, Douglas and Moore, Robert. *King, Warrior, Magician, Lover: Rediscovering the Archetypes of the Mature Masculine*, 1991.

Campbell, Joseph. *The Hero with a Thousand Faces*, 1949.

Hulse, Elliot. *King: The 4 Layer Approach to Becoming the Strongest Version of Yourself*, 2016.

Osho. *Tantra: The Supreme Understanding*, 1975.

Osho. *Compassion: The Ultimate Flowering of Love*, 2006.

Arava, Douglas and Chia, Mantak. *The Multi-Orgasmic Man*, 1996.

Biddulph, Steve. *Manhood*, 2004.

Hill, Napoleon. *Think & Grow Rich*, 1937.

Covey, Stephen. *7 Habits of Highly Effective People*, 1989.

Whitecloud, William. *The Magician's Way: What It Really Takes to Find Your Treasure*, 2004.

Jodorowsky, Alejandro. *Psychomagic: The Transformative Power of Shamanic Psychotherapy*, 1995.

Armstrong, Alison. *Keys to the Kingdom*, 2003.

Deida, David. *Wild Nights*, 2000.

Brown, Michael. *The Presence Process*, 2005.

Florence, Vanessa. *Dancing Eros*. 2018

Estés, Clarissa Pinkola. *Women Who Run With the Wolves*, 1992.

Tomas, Dane. *Clear Your Shit*, 2015.

MORE ABOUT DANE:

Dane has been working with masculine and feminine energy, emotional conditioning and researching consciousness and human evolution committedly since 2001.

He's created a number of programs for unpacking emotional baggage, for training conscious entrepreneurs and for assisting men to more deeply integrate and develop themselves.

You can find out more about these programs below.

The Integrated Man Online Archetype Challenge

This online challenge has been designed to perfectly accompany this book–so if you want me to walk you through the process of initiating yourself into each archetype so that you can rapidly level up as a lover, as a leader, as a human being and as a man–I built this for you. This program will contain all the practical stuff that's hard to include in a book and will allow you to share the journey with other men also on the same path. Best of all, it's only $47 so it's affordable for everyone!

www.theintegratedman.com

The Spiral

The Spiral is Dane's signature process for clearing emotional baggage and allowing people to step into their full power and authentic self-expression. It's a 7 stage process, that delves into the 22 emotions common to human experience in order to free people from the patterns accumulated during childhood.

Find out more at:

www.thespiral.com

Clear Your Shit

Clear Your Shit is a free video training (accompanied by the book of the same name, which you can find on Amazon) that teaches you how to clear your own emotional blocks in seconds.

Enroll here at:

www.clearyourshit.com

To learn more about any of the above or to contact Dane for interviews/ podcasts/public talks/articles etc. please email contact@Danetomas.com

ACKNOWLEDGMENTS:

Massive gratitude to everyone who's ever taught me anything about being a man and how to get where I want to go in life. There's no way I'll name everyone but lemme give it a shot.

To my Dad–Edward Newton–thank you for being an amazing father. I learned more from you than I'll ever be able to tell you. I love you.

To Vanessa Florence. You, and the mystical parallel journey of masculine and feminine work we've been on, is woven all through this book. You made me not only want to be a better man but create a whole fucking system and pathway for others to do it too. That's kind of a big deal. I'm forever grateful for the impact you've had on me. I love you.

To my brothers.

I'm so fucking grateful for all of you!

James Skalkos. Alex White. Chuck Mayfield. James Looker. Karl Edmondson. Uwe Jacobs. Dave Thompson. Ash Lilley. Zulu Flow. Rhyn Nasser. Tom Kippenberger. Adam Sowden. Reece Nugent. Eyal Matisliah. Mark Robinson. Charlie Van Der Lit. Sebastien Daka. Brad Sims.

Shout out to EVERYONE who did the original Integrated Man courses back in 2014 too!

To my teachers and fellow leaders near and far.

John Demartini. Shantam Nityama. Janine Maree. David Deida. Robert Bly. Michaela Boehm. Emma Power. Susan Santoro (that quote!). Shaney Marie Lioness. Sea Song. Laura Deva. Ohad Pele. Alice Hammerle. Steve Biddulph. Elliot Hulse. Shae Matthews. Seth Ananda. James Marshall. Liam McRae.

Thank you to everyone who supports me and my work and thank you to everyone who gets triggered by me or challenges me and forces me to reconsider my thoughts and ideas.

Made in the USA
Las Vegas, NV
03 July 2021

25875654R00069